OVERCOMING ADVERSITY:
SHARING THE AMERICAN DREAM

CHUCK NORRIS

MASON CREST PUBLISHERS
PHILADELPHIA

OVERCOMING ADVERSITY:
SHARING THE AMERICAN DREAM

OVERCOMING ADVERSITY:
SHARING THE AMERICAN DREAM

CHUCK NORRIS

AL HEMINGWAY

MASON CREST PUBLISHERS
PHILADELPHIA

ABOUT CROSS-CURRENTS

When you see this logo, turn to the Cross-Currents section at the back of the book. The Cross-Currents features explore connections between people, places, events, and ideas.

Produced by OTTN Publishing, Stockton, New Jersey

Mason Crest Publishers
370 Reed Road
Broomall, PA 19008
www.masoncrest.com

First printing

1 3 5 7 9 8 6 4 2

Library of Congress Cataloging-in-Publication Data

Hemingway, Albert, 1950-
  Chuck Norris / Al Hemingway.
      p. cm. — (Sharing the American dream)
  Includes bibliographical references and index.
  ISBN 978-1-4222-0591-4 (hardcover)
  ISBN 978-1-4222-0758-1 (pbk.)
  1. Norris, Chuck, 1940-   —Juvenile literature. 2. Martial artists—United States—
Biography—Juvenile literature. 3. Actors—United States—Biography—Juvenile literature.
I. Title.
  GV1113.N67H46 2008
  796.8092—dc22
                        2008024459

TABLE OF CONTENTS

CHAPTER ONE

ACCOMPLISHMENT

Chuck Norris has won countless martial arts championships—including one in 1968 during which he fought with a broken jaw! His martial arts schools have turned out many black-belt champions. And his fighting skill made him a Hollywood superstar.

There is a softer side, though, to the hard-hitting image Norris created for himself in the movies and television. Chuck Norris believes children are the future. He has devoted himself to giving them the tools they need to succeed in life.

Norris always enjoyed teaching kids martial arts. The sport builds self-esteem, discipline, and confidence. He feels these qualities help kids stay away from drugs, alcohol, and other problems in order to lead more productive lives.

Chuck Norris was a successful instructor. But Norris could only reach a few children that way. He wanted to do something on a wider scale. He wanted thousands of kids to be able to learn the benefits of martial arts.

Lunch with the President

Norris received a surprise phone call in 1988. George Herbert Walker Bush, the vice president at the time, was running for

Chuck Norris is known for his tough-guy image and his fighting skill. However, over the years he has used his celebrity to help others in many different ways.

president. Bush's campaign manager, Lee Atwater, asked if Norris would help on the campaign trail. Norris quickly accepted. He appeared at rallies and gave speeches supporting the Republican candidate.

After Bush won the election, Norris became a frequent guest at the White House. One day at lunch, he told President Bush his idea—teaching martial arts to kids in public schools. Bush asked how it could be done. "I said that I felt martial arts classes could be offered as an elective," Norris later described in his autobiography *Against All Odds: My Story*, "as an alternative to regular physical education classes." Norris went on to share his calculations. If there were five classes with 30 kids each, he pointed out to Bush, then 150 kids could be taught each day in each school.

Bush loved the idea. He gave Norris names of people who could help him set up the program. After months of visiting government and business officials, the program began to take shape.

A Kick Start for Kids

The Kick Drugs Out of America Foundation (KDOA) started on August 16, 1990. Norris served as chairman. The nonprofit group focused on the area around Houston, Texas. Houston was not far from where Norris had a ranch, and President Bush also had strong ties to Texas. KDOA chose to begin the program in the M.C. Williams Middle School, a large urban school.

Norris had a hectic film schedule. He needed a strong person to run the course. He chose Roy White. White had a black belt in karate and would be a good teacher. Several weeks later, White called Norris. He was concerned about the

READ MORE

What are martial arts? Find out more on page 44.

President George H.W. Bush wears a *gi*, a martial arts uniform, while attending a karate exhibition with Chuck Norris (red shirt) at an anti-drug program in Houston, 1992.

school they had chosen. He said the students were rowdy and disrespectful. He did not think the program could succeed there. Norris asked White to continue until he returned. Then they could both figure out what to do.

Norris came to visit the school four months later. When he walked into the gym, he was surprised. He saw 150 children in karate uniforms welcoming him back! Norris spoke with them all and answered their questions. Then the students staged a martial arts exhibition. They wanted to show him what they had been taught.

White later told Norris that he knew he needed to help the students change their negative attitudes to positive ones. As the days passed, the children began to respond to his encouragement. White even sparred with the roughest kid in the school. By the end of the session, the student was calling him "Mr. White" and "sir." It looked like White's work had paid off. KDOA would be a success. Norris's dream of reaching out to more children was now a reality.

The organization changed its name to KickStart in 2003. The program now deals the growing problem of gangs in schools. "A sense of belonging is an integral part of everyone's life," the official KickStart website states, "and many of the inner city children turn to gang-related groups because they feel they fit in nowhere else. The Foundation offers them a positive alternative. When students join the program, they earn the right to belong to the Chuck Norris T.E.A.M.–'T' for truth, 'E' for esteem, 'A' for attitude, 'M' for motivation."

KickStart has become part of the curriculum in more than 40 schools in Texas. More than 50,000 students have participated. Norris created a program that helps kids learn how to do something they enjoy. At the same time, it helps address one of the most serious issues facing today's cities and towns— the growing problem of gangs. Although he has been showered with many awards over the years, Norris believes this is his most rewarding accomplishment.

READ MORE

Gang activity is on the rise in many cities and towns across the country. To find out more about this very serious problem, see page 45.

The Secret of Success

Children often ask Chuck Norris about the secret of his success. He says there is no magic formula. He feels that a positive attitude and an old-fashioned work ethic are the keys to a rewarding life.

His can-do attitude has helped Norris accomplish many of his goals. For example, because he was older when he tried to become an actor, he was told that he would never make it in

Hollywood. "If I had accepted such judgments," Norris explains in *Against All Odds*, "I would never have made that first movie; nor would I have persisted and made other films after the first. I treated the initial rejections as temporary setbacks because I knew that with enough time, determination, and hard work— along with a faith in God and a positive mental attitude— I would succeed."

Chuck Norris's strong will has helped him conquer his problems and achieve his goals. Although he was born and raised in poverty and had a difficult childhood, this did not stop him from accomplishing the things he set out to do. He wants to pass this lesson on to future generations. He has become a positive role model to countless kids across this nation.

CHAPTER TWO

A CORE OF STRENGTH

E ven as a baby, Chuck Norris had to fight to survive. He had trouble breathing after he was born on March 10, 1940. For days he was fed with an eyedropper until he could be released from the hospital.

Wilma and Ray Norris named their new son Carlos Ray Norris. "Carlos" was the name of their minister in the family's hometown of Ryan, Oklahoma. He did not get the nickname "Chuck" until much later, when he was serving in the Air Force. To this day, Norris's close friends and family call him Carlos.

As the years passed, the small family grew. A brother named Wieland was born in 1943. Aaron followed in 1951. Norris rarely saw his father, an alcoholic womanizer who was often looking for work. The family moved 13 times before Norris turned 15.

Norris spent many hours at the movies. He watched cowboy stars like John Wayne and Gary Cooper. He looked up to them for their integrity and honesty. Norris saw men like them as male role models in place of his alcoholic and abusive father.

Norris was raised primarily by his mother and grandmother. His mother provided him with love and guidance. He credits her with much of his later success. "She was the most positive influ-

Chuck Norris as a senior at North Torrance High School.

ence in my life," he wrote in *The Secret of Inner Strength: My Story*, "and she taught my brother and me to never think of the bad, but only of the good, and to do what had to be done without complaint. That philosophy of hers became an integral part of my life and the core of my inner strength."

School Years

Norris handled any tough chore without complaint. He believes that trait comes from his Native American heritage. (Both of his parents were half Irish and half Cherokee Indian.) In school, however, Norris was very quiet and withdrawn.

Norris's classmates often made ethnic slurs about his Indian background. Bullies also targeted him. The biggest kid in class, a boy named Bobby, chased Norris home from school every day.

A man named Jack owned the house where the Norrises lived. Jack stopped Norris one day and told him he could not keep running. He would have to face Bobby. Realizing that Jack was right, Norris ran and tackled the bully, forcing him to the ground. The two boys fought until the bully cried out for Norris to stop.

READ MORE

For more information about legendary actor John Wayne, turn to page 46.

When the fight was over, the bully never chased Norris again. They even became friends.

This event is still important to Norris. "Confronting Bobby the bully taught me an important lesson about fear," he wrote in *Against All Odds*. "It can often be overcome simply by facing it."

A Positive Male Role Model

Norris's parents divorced in 1956. The breakup was painful, but Wilma Norris believed it had to be done. She moved to California with the boys, first to Gardena and then to the city of Torrance.

Wilma found a job at a nearby Northrop Aircraft plant. In 1957, she married a kind and caring man named George Knight, a foreman at Northrop. Norris and his new stepfather developed a close relationship. "I discovered a new pride in myself, too," he said in *Against All Odds*, "and began to blossom,

READ MORE

Chuck Norris is part Cherokee. To learn more about the Cherokee people, see page 47.

Chuck (number 1) is in the center of this photo of his high school football team, circa 1957. Chuck worked hard to make the team, even though he was not a starter.

thanks to our family unity and a strong paternal influence." Norris finally had the father figure he had wanted all his life.

When Norris entered high school, George encouraged him to try to join the football team. Norris worked very hard to make the team. "I was shy, unathletic and only a C student," he later said. "I did make the football team, but I was second string. The coach wanted those aggressive types. I just wasn't one of them."

At that time, no one could have guessed that one day Chuck Norris would be famous around the world as a fighter. But step by step, the shy little boy was growing up to be a confident young man.

Turning Point

While going to North Torrance High School, Norris met and fell in love with Dianne Holechek. They dated during their senior year. At that time, Norris's dream was to become a police officer. He thought he could get experience in law enforcement by entering the military.

In August of 1958, Norris enlisted in the U.S. Air Force. That December, he and Dianne got married. He was 18 and she was 17. Within a year, Norris was transferred to Osan Air Force Base in South Korea for a year. He was sad to be separated from his wife, but he had no choice. Little did he realize that his tour of duty there would change his life forever.

While in South Korea, Norris enrolled in the judo club on base. During one class, he broke his collarbone. But he was still determined to learn judo. As he walked through Osan village one day, he saw some local people practicing tang soo do. This is a Korean form of karate that later became associated with tae kwon do. Norris was amazed. He wanted to know how to maneuver

Chuck and his wife, Dianne, circa 1975. The high school sweethearts were married six months after Chuck graduated from high school.

and fight like them. Norris described this period of his life in his book *The Secret Power Within: Zen Solutions to Real Problems:*

> Looking back, I realize that was *the* turning point in my life, because it was while I was in Osan, Korea, that I started to study martial arts. For the first time I began to see at least part of my childhood dream as a possible reality, and I had a consuming passion to learn something, although I had no idea then where it would lead. But, as the Zen masters say, the longest journey begins with the first step, and, unknowingly, I had taken the first step leading to my future.

Norris worked hard and learned quickly. By the time his year in Osan ended, Norris was a certified black belt in tang soo do. By achieving that goal, Norris's self-esteem skyrocketed. He had taken on a very difficult task—and had mastered it.

CHAPTER THREE

MARTIAL ARTS MASTER

After returning from South Korea, Norris served as a military policeman at the March Air Force Base in California. He was discharged from the air force in 1962. He then became a filing clerk at the Northrop plant, where his mother worked. Norris also added his name to the waiting list to take the test for the Los Angeles Police Department. Another major event in Norris's life occurred in 1962 as well. Norris's wife Dianne gave birth to their first child, Mike, in October.

To help earn more money, Norris started teaching karate lessons in his parents' backyard. He taught his brothers the sport. Soon more people wanted to learn.

Norris borrowed $600 to open his first karate studio. He started in Torrance with 10 students. Norris's work schedule often kept him busy until late in the evening. As his reputation as a gifted instructor spread, he opened another studio. In 1964, he left the Northrop plant to teach karate full-time. He knew he had a family to support, which would be harder to do without the security of his full-time factory job. Still, he felt he had to do what he loved.

Norris also entered his first karate tournament in 1964, along with three of his students. They drove together to Salt Lake

Utah, for the event. Norris won his first two contests but lost the third fight. His opponent had watched his other matches and knew how to counter his moves. Norris described the ride home in *Against All Odds*:

> The matches were hotly contested, but when the smoke from the heavy competition cleared, my three students had won and I had lost. I was still smarting within as I drove all the way back to Los Angeles, my students clinging to their trophies and exuberantly reliving the highlights of their victorious matches. Meanwhile I mulled over how I had lost. I decided then and there, I may lose another tournament, but I'll never lose the same way twice.

On His Way Up

True to his word, Norris never lost a match the same way again. And as his fame grew, so did his family. His second son, Eric, was born in 1964. Norris kept entering competitions, winning various titles in California. He also studied with several different teachers, picking up skills from other martial arts to include in his fighting.

In 1967, Norris traveled to New York's Madison Square Garden. He defeated 13 challengers, representing every weight class, in an amazing 11 hours. His reward? The All-American Grand Championship trophy! Exhausted, Norris headed back to his hotel room. On the way, legendary martial arts

Chuck delivers one of his signature kicks for the camera. From 1968 to 1974, Chuck was undefeated as a professional middleweight karate competitor, winning the world championship six times.

champion Bruce Lee congratulated him. From that talk, the pair became good friends. Norris was on his way to the top of the martial arts field.

Success

What does it take to deliver a kick while flying five feet in the air? Not one time, but every time? What is involved in mastering the spinning back kick—until it becomes your trademark? Or perfecting the roundhouse? It is the same as with any skill. "The key here is practice," Norris wrote in his book *Winning Tournament Karate*, "a constant repetition that will improve your timing and most important of all, render your attacks reflexive. If practiced properly, you will not need to think during a match, but simply act and react."

READ MORE

Bruce Lee is credited with starting the martial arts movie craze in America. To learn more about him, see page 48.

It seems Chuck Norris mastered that ability. Through the rest of 1967, Norris was undefeated and won more than 30 tournaments altogether. One of these was the International Grand Championship, when he defeated former boxing champion Joe Lewis in the final match.

Norris achieved even greater success the next year. He was Grand Champion at the Internationals again, and also became the Professional World Middleweight Karate Champion. Norris held that title from 1968 until he retired from competition in 1974.

A Terrible Loss

This was an exciting period in Chuck Norris's martial arts career. At the same time, though, the United States was in an upheaval because of war in South Vietnam. Both of Norris's brothers, Wieland and Aaron, enlisted in the U.S. Army. Aaron was sent to South Korea. Wieland was ordered to Vietnam. While serving with the famous 101st Airborne Division at Firebase Ripcord on June 3, 1970, Wieland was killed by enemy fire.

Norris was devastated. "I know why he was in Vietnam," he later wrote in *The Secret Power Within: Zen Solutions to Real Problems*. "After all, he and I, along with Aaron, grew up together, learning and discussing the same ideals, which included patriotism and the willingness to give all we had for our country. He died doing the right thing, making the right gesture: going ahead alone to make the way safe for the men who were depending on him."

More Changes

In addition to his brother's death, there were other changes in store for Chuck Norris. He and his business partner, Bob Wall, decided to sell their martial arts schools to a large company in 1970. After the sale, they agreed to stay on as instructors in exchange for 2 percent of the profits. During the early 1970s, Norris began teaching martial arts to celebrities, including Steve McQueen, Michael Landon, Donny and Marie Osmond, and Priscilla Presley.

As Chuck Norris's career took off, his family was growing as well. In this mid-1970s photo, Chuck and Dianne Norris are pictured with their sons, 12-year-old Mike and 10-year-old Eric, at their California home.

Norris continued developing his own martial arts style to teach to his students. It was based on his training in tang soo do, but included elements from other traditions as well. Norris used different names for it over the years, finally choosing chun kuk do, or "the universal way," in 1990. (The Korean phrase literally means "the way of 1000 lands.") Today the United Fighting Arts Federation (UFAF), also founded by Norris, establishes ranking guidelines and standards for teaching chun kuk do. The UFAF also hosts annual world championship tournaments in the discipline.

In the meantime, though, Norris had other adventures headed his way. He traveled to Europe and Hong Kong in 1972 to appear in *Return of the Dragon*, a movie that starred his friend Bruce Lee. The two men fought an amazing fight scene in the movie that has since become a classic. (Even today that scene

Chuck Norris (left) battles martial arts legend Bruce Lee in a scene from *Return of the Dragon.*

can be found on YouTube.com.) Tragically, however, Lee died before the U.S. release of the film.

Norris received some more bad news after his return from Hong Kong. His biological father—whom he had not seen in years—had been killed in an automobile accident. Norris and his brother Aaron went to the funeral in Oklahoma. "For the first time in a long while, I couldn't help wondering what an empty life our dad must have known," he later said in *Against All Odds*. "I determined in my heart and mind that I wanted to be there for my kids." Even though Norris's relationship with his father had been difficult, this was a very sad time for him.

Retirement

By 1973, the karate schools Norris started in 1964 were struggling. They had gone through several owners who had no real interest in them. To help prevent the schools from going into bankruptcy, Norris bought them back. He later found out that the business owed more taxes than he had realized. Norris did everything he could

READ MORE

Some martial arts are very popular. Find out more on page 49.

to raise the money. Though that task seemed impossible, in the end he was able to sell his schools again to pay off the debts.

Norris had always relied on the strong values he learned from his mother. They pulled him through these rough times as well.

In 1974, Norris decided to officially retire as a professional martial arts competitor. He had won many trophies and awards, including his undefeated middleweight title. However, he felt that there was less respect in the competitions. He believed the time was right to retire from the sport he loved—as a winner.

A New Career

His karate schools had been sold, and his competitive days were behind him. Though he would continue to teach martial arts as a private instructor, Norris wondered what to do next. His friend Steve McQueen—a famous actor himself, who was known as the "king of Cool"—suggested acting. "You've got this intensity in your eyes when you fight that audiences might find appealing," McQueen reportedly told him. "Could be profitable for you."

A world-class martial arts champion can just walk into Hollywood and become a star, right? Not so fast. Norris had tried acting a few times in small roles and felt uncomfortable. Besides, there were 16,000 struggling actors in Hollywood at that time. What chance would he have? Still, McQueen told him to give it a try. Norris signed up for acting school to improve his skills.

His first major role in a Hollywood film was in the 1977 movie *Breaker! Breaker!* The film was about a trucker who fights corruption in a small town. Norris got a modest salary for his part. He kept looking for other acting jobs.

But Norris had some ideas of his own, as well. He and a fellow black belt had worked on an outline about a former U.S. Army Special Forces member whose friends are being killed off one by one. He must find out why before he is next. Norris and his partner took their rough script for *Good Guys Wear Black* to a friend who was a professional writer. He wrote a short screenplay from the outline. Norris liked it and started looking for financial investors to back his movie.

Norris's status as a martial arts expert and world karate champion did give him access to Hollywood producers. However, his lack of acting ability hurt his chances to get his screenplay made into a movie. For more than three years, Norris literally carried his script door-to-door trying to convince people to invest in his idea. Finally, a group of investors with a brand-new company called American Cinema took a chance on the script.

The Coach Gets Coached

Because Norris did not have much acting experience, American Cinema hired Jonathan Harris as his voice coach. Harris had acted in many television shows. He was probably best known as the evil Dr. Zachary Smith on *Lost in Space*, a science fiction television series that ran from 1965 to 1968.

Harris spent three weeks teaching Norris the right way to pronounce his dialogue. Harris used an unusual method to get Norris to open his mouth wide enough when he was speaking. He simply placed his fingers in Norris's mouth and stretched it—much to Norris's surprise.

Good Guys Wear Black was released in June of 1978. It was a huge success, grossing $18 million. Norris's next film, *A Force of One*, came out in 1979. It made more than $20 million. In 1980, *The Octagon* gave Norris another box office hit.

Norris's fame, and income, rose dramatically. Following the advice of McQueen—who told him to work on his screen presence and keep his dialogue to a minimum—Norris was on his way to becoming a genuine Hollywood box office draw. Once again, he had started something from scratch. And once again, he was rising to the top.

CHAPTER FOUR

TRAGEDY—AND SUCCESS

In the early 1980s, action films like *An Eye for an Eye, Silent Rage,* and *Lone Wolf McQuade* put Chuck Norris's career on the upswing. Moviegoers loved his hard-hitting films. They considered Chuck Norris to be in the same class as other action heroes, such as Charles Bronson, Clint Eastwood, and Sylvester Stallone.

With several successful movies under his belt, Norris pursued an idea that was important to him. He had always wanted to do a movie about the Vietnam War. He hoped to honor the memory of his brother and others who served there. However, at the time, Vietnam was not a popular subject. Few people in Hollywood were interested in a film about the conflict and its veterans.

Norris would not take no for an answer. He had a script about American servicemen still being held in Vietnam. The major production companies wanted no part of such a risky project. They felt that the public was still uneasy about the war.

READ MORE

The Vietnam War was a major turning point in American history. To learn more about it, see page 50.

A scene from *Missing in Action,* starring Chuck as an Army colonel determined to save American soldiers being held as prisoners of war in Vietnam. The 1984 film was one of the biggest hits of Chuck's career.

Finally, Cannon Films agreed to make the picture. The title was *Missing in Action.* The plot centered around Norris's character, U.S. Army Colonel James Braddock. He returns to Vietnam to free prisoners of war.

Near Death

Missing in Action was shot in the Philippines, where the terrain resembles the jungles of Vietnam. The action scenes were dangerous. One of them nearly cost Norris his life. He was supposed to be pulled out of a river by helicopter after saving a group of prisoners. He would then be lowered back down again. Somehow there was a misunderstanding. The chopper took off and never lowered him back into the water. Norris was dangling from a ladder 300 feet in the air. The pilot had no idea he was there!

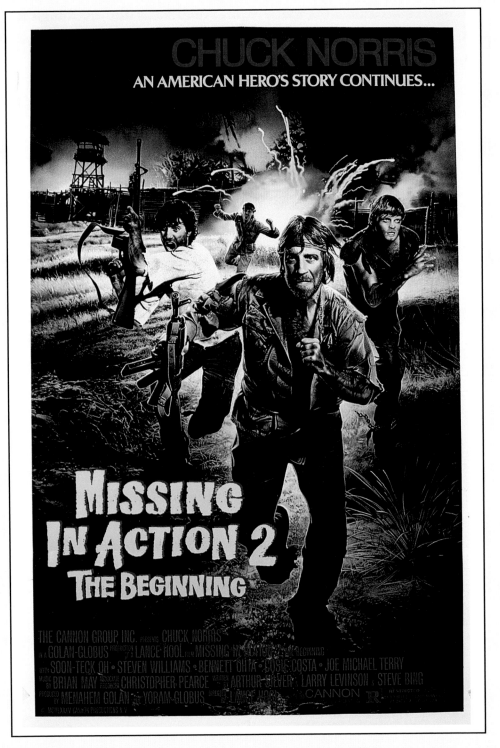

Promotional poster for *Missing in Action 2: The Beginning* (1985).

Norris's brother, who was a stunt coordinator for the film, rushed to his rescue. "Aaron jumped into a boat and started chasing after us as the helicopter swooped out over the ocean," Norris related in *Against All Odds*. "Meanwhile, the assistant director radioed the pilot, who had no idea that I was still hanging on. He swung the bird around and lowered me onto the beach. The guys on the ground had to pry my fingers off the ladder."

When *Missing in Action* was released in 1984, it was an immediate hit. In the first week alone it grossed $6 million. It was even well-received by critics who usually panned Norris's movies and his stiff acting style. Norris normally took their criticism in stride. It was the viewing audience's praise that meant the most to him. Still, he was pleased that the critics seemed to enjoy this film.

Cannon Films was excited by the success of *Missing in Action*. The following year, they released a prequel, *Missing in Action 2: The Beginning*. It depicted Braddock's original capture, imprisonment, and escape from a prison camp. This was followed in 1988 with a sequel to the other two called *Braddock: Missing in Action III*.

Toughest Scene Ever

During the filming of *Missing in Action 2: The Beginning*, Norris had to perform a very difficult scene. His character James Braddock has been captured. One of his follow prisoners suffers from malaria, but the commander will only give him medicine on one condition. Braddock must sign a paper saying he committed war crimes against the Vietnamese. Reluctantly, he signs. The head of the camp, however, had no intention of helping. Instead he has the prisoner burned alive. Braddock must witness his friend's execution.

To evoke the passion needed for the scene, Norris thought of his brother Wieland in Vietnam. He imagined him being killed by the enemy. His thoughts also drifted to his brother's funeral. He pictured Wieland's body in the casket at the funeral home. These gut wrenching images had the necessary effect on Norris. The effort left him emotionally drained, however. He vowed he would never act in such a scene again.

Critics and Audiences Take Notice

With tough scenes like the one in *Missing in Action 2*, Norris began to mature as an actor. More movie roles poured in for the once-shy kid from Oklahoma. He starred in 1985's *Invasion USA* and *Code of Silence*, both money-makers. *Code of Silence* also won more good reviews for Norris. "*Code of Silence* is a thriller so professional that it has the confidence to go for drama and humor as well as thrills," wrote film critic Roger Ebert. "It may be the movie that moves Norris out of the ranks of dependable action heroes and makes him a major star."

READ MORE

Delta Force is an actual unit within the U.S. armed forces. To find out more, see page 51.

In 1986, Norris starred in *Firewalker* as well as *The Delta Force*. The latter was based on a true story about an elite unit ordered into Beirut, Lebanon, after an American plane was hijacked by terrorists. Audiences loved it, and Norris's fame soared.

His character, Colonel Scot McCoy, was back in action again for the 1990 sequel, *Delta Force 2: The Colombian Connection* (also known as *Delta Force 2: Operation Stranglehold*). In the film McCoy and a group of commandos set out to rescue hostages from a drug lord before they are executed.

In *Firewalker* (1986), Chuck starred with Melody Anderson and Louis Gossett Jr. The film about treasure hunting in Central America gave Chuck a chance to mix some comic lines with his usual punches and kicks. His acting received mostly good reviews.

Delta Force 2 was shown at the famous Senate Theater in Washington, D.C., before its national release. Hundreds of people attended, including several politicians. Sitting in the front row with Norris and his brother Aaron were Republican senators Bob Dole and Pete Wilson. Dole told Norris that they would not be able to stay. He and Wilson were expected back to the Senate chambers for an important vote.

As the pair prepared to leave, Norris thanked them for coming. A few minutes later, Norris happened to turn around. He saw both men in the back of the theater, still watching the film. Dole and Wilson were so involved in the movie that they were late for the vote!

Too Much Violence?

Norris cares most about the reaction of his fans, not his critics. When his *Missing in Action* films were released, Norris received thousands of letters from people praising him for not being afraid to tackle the subject of the Vietnam War. One daughter of a Vietnam veteran wrote that her father cried while watching it.

Others, however, have questioned the violence in his movies. Critics think it is harmful for young people to watch.

Chuck Norris has argued that his films do not promote gratuitous violence. He has said that they illustrate the theme of good against evil, with the good guy always winning in the end. In his movies, he only used his martial arts skills as a last resort. He has said that his characters are molded after his childhood heroes, especially John Wayne, who displayed honor and truthfulness when confronted with difficult situations.

Norris has commented on the subject of violence in his movies many times. "I don't like violence for violence's sake," he told *New York Times* writer Ira Berkow. "In my movies, I never attack anyone. I don't cause trouble, but I end it." Norris—who generally has a very quiet and peaceful personality—also rejected the idea of an overly-macho or violent approach to real-life situations. "I'm not Superman," he continued later in the interview. "If a guy comes up behind me and puts a gun to my back and tells me to give him my wallet, what I'd do is reach back, pull out my wallet and give it to him. Absolutely. You'd be foolish to gamble your life for money."

Divorce, and a New Beginning

In 1989, Norris and his wife Dianne divorced. Their careers had taken them in different directions, and they now had little in common. Though it was not an easy decision, they parted on friendly terms.

Still, the trauma of the separation weighed heavily on Norris. He buried himself in his work. He even took up hobbies such as truck and boat racing to forget his troubles. He once raced a 46-foot Scarab power boat more than 600 miles in just over 12 hours, breaking a record for that distance by 26 minutes. Norris had to quit his hazardous hobby, though, when a producer at Cannon Films heard about it. Norris had signed on to do more films, and the company did not want anything to happen to him.

Norris made several films in the early 1990s. He tried to portray a character with a darker side in *The Hitman*. Unfortunately, it did not work, and critics gave the 1991 film bad reviews. This was followed by *Sidekicks* in 1992, which did not fare well with the critics or at the box office.

These two flops did not deter Chuck Norris. He was approached to do a television series. The main character would be a modern-day Texas Ranger who uses his expertise in martial arts to fight criminals. It would be a huge risk. Not all movie actors can make the difficult transition to television. Norris also understood that making a television series could be very demanding. Although hesitant, Norris took the role. He would never regret the decision.

A scene from *Sidekicks* (1992), a comedy-action film in which Chuck helps a young man fight back against some bullies. Unfortunately, the film flopped at the box office.

CHAPTER FIVE

A NEW SHOW AND A NEW LIFE

In 1993, Chuck Norris began filming episodes of *Walker, Texas Ranger*. CBS aired the show on Saturday night, usually a tough slot. But when the series premiered on April 21, 1993, the public loved it. Norris fans did not have to wait anymore to see him at the movies. They could watch him on television, from the comfort of their own living rooms.

The series had a good supporting cast. It also included a love interest for Walker, the character of female Assistant District Attorney Alex Cahill, played by Sheree J. Wilson. Norris and his brother Aaron became the show's executive producers.

Walker, Texas Ranger ran for nine seasons. "You had enough action for Dad to sit down and watch, but we didn't step over the boundary where kids couldn't watch," Norris once said. "We worked very hard to find the fine line between action and violence. Of course, the relationship between Walker and Alex brought the women over."

Another great follow-up to the show came later. In 2005, Norris was coaxed by CBS

READ MORE

To find out more about the real-life Texas Rangers, turn to page 52.

Promotional photo from the first season of *Walker, Texas Ranger*, picturing Chuck Norris and his costars, Sheree J. Wilson (left) and Clarence Gilyard. The television series was very popular, running on CBS from 1993 to 2001.

executives to do a two-hour television movie. Norris would return to the role of Cordell Walker. The response to the TV movie was phenomenal. Viewers asked when the next episode would be shown.

Unfortunately, Chuck Norris has a hectic schedule of public appearances and a demanding personal life. Reviving *Walker, Texas Ranger* would be impossible for him. Nonetheless, some diehard Norris fans still wait for the day when he might again put on his cowboy boots and Stetson hat and pin on the badge of a Texas Ranger.

The True Meaning of Courage

In spite of his workload, Norris has always made every attempt to set aside time to spend with children. Aside from his KickStart program, he has volunteered countless hours to many groups that help neglected and deprived kids.

The Make-A-Wish Foundation is one such group. In the mid-1980s, it asked Norris to assist them in helping Michael Majia, who had leukemia. The five-year-old boy from California was a huge Chuck Norris fan. His wish was for an autographed photo of his hero.

Norris was elated. He volunteered to drive to Michael's home and hand him the picture in person. Majia's favorite film was *Lone Wolf McQuade,* which he watched continuously. The two became fast friends at their first meeting. Norris invited Michael and his parents to his private movie screenings. He even taught Michael some of his karate moves.

READ MORE

For more information about the Make-A-Wish foundation and how it helps children with terminal illnesses, turn to page 53.

When Norris heard that Michael passed away, he was grief-stricken. Michael had succumbed to the dreaded disease while viewing *Lone Wolf McQuade* and clutching Norris's photograph. He was just seven years old.

Majia's death had a profound impact on Norris. He did quite a bit of soul searching and reached some conclusions about his own life and where it was going. Today, he is a devoted advocate of the Make-A-Wish Foundation. He continues to give guidance and support to many children suffering from serious illnesses.

As Cordell "Cord" Walker, Chuck portrayed a tough lawman with a good heart. Just like in real life, Chuck's character on *Walker, Texas Ranger* worked with kids from troubled neighborhoods, speaking to them about the importance of avoiding drugs and staying out of gangs.

Unexpected Joy

A few years after his experience with Michael Majia, Norris was confronted with another kind of earth-shattering news. He received word from a young woman named Dianna (Dina) DeCioli that she was his daughter. Just before his discharge from the U.S. Air Force, Norris had an affair with a woman named Johanna. He ended the relationship and never saw her again. Norris did not realize that she later had a child. Dina had since discovered that Norris was her biological father.

In 1998, Chuck married Gina O'Kelley. He later wrote about the impact falling in love with her has had on his life: "If your whole life is spent trying to make money and you neglect the people important in your life, you will create an emptiness deep in your heart and soul. I know. I fell into that trap. I dedicated my whole life to fame and fortune. I had a huge hole in my heart and was miserable until I met my wife, Gena, who brought me back to the Lord."

Dina sent Norris a letter explaining that she was grown up and married with children of her own. She needed answers about his medical background for her children's benefit. She read that he had divorced and felt it was time to contact him. If he did not answer her note, she would not trouble him anymore.

Norris's mother Wilma wanted to talk with Dina. A meeting was arranged at Wilma's house in 1991. After discussing the delicate situation, Wilma called her son and told him to come over immediately. As he drove to his mother's home, Norris kept asking himself how he would know if Dina really was his daughter. When the two first met, though, there was no doubt in his mind that she was his child. "I went to her," he wrote in *Against All Odds*, "wrapped my arms around her, and we both started crying. At that moment it was if I had known her all of her life."

Norris's other children accepted Dina as part of their family. And while Norris was ashamed about having an extramarital affair, Dina was a blessing to him.

A New Love

Every aspect of Chuck Norris's life was going well. He was a famous celebrity in both movies and television. He had three wonderful children and nine grandchildren that kept him very busy.

But there was still a void in his personal life. After divorcing he had dated, and once almost married, but broke off the engagement. *Walker, Texas Ranger* took up much of his time, with little left over for social events.

That all changed when he met and fell in love with Gena O'Kelley. Gena was a deputy sheriff and part-time model from Chester, California. She also had two children from a previous marriage. Her daughter Kelley was 13, and her son Tim was 10. Both Norris and Gena knew they would have to be accepted by each other's family. It was not going to be a simple task. Also,

Gena had a strong Christian faith. Partly because of her influence, Norris's own faith was renewed.

Before their wedding, Norris went to Gena's son and asked for his consent. He remembered that his own mother had asked him if she should marry George Knight so many years ago. Tim agreed. Now Norris would know how it felt to be a stepfather. It took a long time before Gena's children felt completely comfortable with the situation. But eventually they all grew close as a family.

On November 28, 1998, Chuck and Gena were wed in Carrolton, Texas. They exchanged vows as country-western singer Sammy Kershaw sang their wedding song, "You Are the Love of My Life." Chuck Norris's life was entering yet another a new phase.

A New Surprise

Norris now had a large family. The thought of having more children at his age had never entered his mind. But many of his friends told him about the joy they experienced by having children later in life. Chuck and Gena decided to try to have a child after all.

When Gina became pregnant, they were both very happy. Then they learned they would be having twins! But it was not going to be easy. Gena's pregnancy was especially difficult. She needed emergency surgery to save the babies while Norris was attending a presidential dinner in Washington, D.C. Norris flew back to Los Angeles to be by her side.

Finally, after much anxiety and pain, Gena Norris gave birth about two months later on August 30, 2001. Dakota Alan arrived first, followed closely by his sister, Danilee Kelley. Each of them weighed less than five pounds.

Because they were premature births, the twins had to stay in the hospital for around-the-clock care. The staff closely moni-

Chuck signs an autograph for a U.S. Marine while visiting a military base in Iraq, 2007. The movie star has spoken often about the importance of supporting American troops.

tored their breathing and other vital signs. After four weeks, the new parents brought the babies home. Nurses stayed with them to provide additional care for the twins.

The birth of his son and daughter filled the emptiness in Norris's heart. He felt alive again. They also helped bring Chuck and Gena's older children closer together. "Danilee and Dakota have become the glue that binds our two families together," he remarked in *Against All Odds*.

A Very Busy Life

In addition to the time he has spent working and with his family, Chuck Norris is also a writer. He wrote a martial arts guide in 1975, *Winning Tournament Karate*. Several other books have followed more recently. In 2004, he co-authored *Against All Odds: My Story* with writer Ken Abraham. It was a follow-up to his 1988 book *The Secret of Inner Strength: My Story*. His book *Black Belt Patriotism: How to Reawaken America* came out in 2008. Norris has even tried his hand at fiction. He and a team of writers—including his brother Aaron and Ken Abraham—created the Justice Riders series, publishing two novels in 2006 and 2007. He also has earned writing and producing credits for some of his movies and television shows.

A political conservative, Norris endorsed Republicans George H.W. Bush and George W. Bush for president. For the 2008 election, he campaigned on behalf of presidential hopeful Mike

Chuck stands on stage at a rally in New Hampshire while Mike Hukabee speaks to supporters. During the 2008 presidential campaign, Chuck was a strong supporter of Huckabee, a former governor of Arkansas.

Huckabee of Arkansas. Senator John McCain, however, won the Republican nomination. On November 4, 2008, McCain was defeated by Democratic candidate Barack Obama, the first African American ever elected president of the United States.

Throughout his martial arts career and his time in Hollywood, Norris has been given many honors and awards. It is his humanitarian side, though, that many of his fans love. Norris always finds time to visit veterans hospitals and the troops in Iraq and Afghanistan. Since the 1980s, he has been actively involved with the Make-a-Wish Foundation for terminally ill children. He made a commercial to help raise money for the United Way, an organization that helps improve communities across the country. Norris has also given motivational talks to various Christian groups across the country.

The characters Chuck Norris has played on screen—instilled with old-fashioned values—are similar to Chuck Norris in real life. The introverted boy from the dust bowl of Oklahoma grew up to play the same kinds of heroes he admired as a child. This quality has inspired his fans, both young and old.

John Wayne would have been proud.

The Martial Arts

The term *martial arts* means "arts of war." There are hundreds of martial arts styles and fighting skills from all around the globe. Asian styles that are popular in the United States include aikido, judo, karate, kendo, tae kwon do, and tai chi chuan. But there are strong traditions in other areas, from Zulu stick fighters in Africa to European boxing and wrestling to American kickboxing. And how about gatka in India, sambo in Russia, and capoeira in Brazil?

Most martial arts include skills such as punching or striking with the hands, kicking, and wrestling or grappling. Some feature weapons. Samurai warriors of Japan often carried two swords—the long, curved katana and the shorter wakizashi.

Japanese ninja were experts in many different kinds of weapons, including the fearsome spiked throwing star. But perhaps the ninja's strongest weapons were stealth and speed, essential qualities for professional assassins.

People may practice martial arts for self-defense, for fitness, to compete, or as a spiritual discipline. That may seem odd. But most martial arts focus on mental as well as physical self-control, and many are linked to spiritual traditions. Several also involve a grading system, often with a black belt or similar distinction for the most accomplished masters.

Today, many young people study martial arts like karate. Mastering martial arts requires both physical training and self-discipline.

The War Against Gangs

Gangs have been a serious and growing problem in the United States for many years, especially in cities and towns. Houston, Texas, is no exception. That is where Chuck Norris started his Kick Drugs Out of America program in 1990. The program's name was changed to KickStart in 2003 after it expanded to help address the problem of gangs.

Groups such as Mara Salvatrucha (MS-13), the Crips, the Bloods, and the Latin Kings are well-established and extremely dangerous gangs. But there are many others. Some may have territories in just one city or neighborhood. What are some of the characteristics of a gang? Typically the group has a name. The members may use certain symbols or colors. Certain hand signs, graffiti styles, and hats or other kinds of clothing may identify a gang member. If you notice this kind of thing happening in your school or neighborhood—or if you see someone carrying weapons or drugs—report it to a teacher or police officer.

In spite of efforts by many groups across the country, gangs continue to be a very serious problem. One of the best ways for at-risk kids to stay out of gangs is to be involved in other groups and activities. Ask a parent, teacher, or other trusted adult in your community if there are groups you can join to help fight the spread of gangs among young people.

Violent street gangs are a growing problem in many American cities.

CROSS-CURRENTS

"The Duke"

Nicknamed "Duke," John Wayne was a hero to many during his long film career. He was born as Marion Michael Morrison in Winterset, Iowa, on May 26, 1907. After attending the University of Southern California on a football scholarship, he worked as a prop boy at Fox Studios. His first starring role was in the western *The Big Trail* in 1930. Director Raoul Walsh did not like his name and changed it to John Wayne.

Wayne made dozens of low budget westerns during the 1930s. But in 1939, John Ford cast him in *Stagecoach*. That was when Hollywood finally took notice of the strapping six-foot-four, 225-pound actor.

Although Wayne played a variety of characters, his best-loved screen roles were in westerns. Films such as *Stagecoach*, *She Wore a Yellow Ribbon*, and *Fort Apache* are classics. He received an Oscar in 1969 for his portrayal of Marshal Rooster Cogburn in the movie *True Grit*. All in all, he made 200 movies in a career that spanned more than 50 years.

John Wayne passed away in 1979 after a long bout with cancer. "He's an American institution and nothing can topple him," said director Andrew McLaglen, who had worked with Wayne on several projects. "He has tremendous guts, he always has. There's the Rock of Gibraltar, the Empire State Building, and Duke Wayne."

John Wayne was one of America's greatest movie stars. To many fans, he became a symbol of American values like toughness, self-reliance, and perseverance.

Trail of Tears

Both of Chuck Norris's parents were half Cherokee Indian. Norris believes his reserved nature and strong will come from his Native American legacy.

Originally, the Cherokees lived in southern Virginia, North Carolina, South Carolina, and Georgia. In 1830, gold was discovered in Georgia. As white settlers moved in, the U.S. government removed the Cherokees from their ancestral homeland. In October 1838, thousands were sent to present-day Oklahoma. Many died along the way because of bad weather and freezing temperatures. On March 26, 1839, the survivors finally reached their destination. This tragic journey became known as the Trail of Tears.

Historically, the Cherokees have been a very proud and advanced people. The same is true today. They are the second largest Indian nation in the United States, with more than 200,000 members living on 7,000 square miles of land. They have their own form of government and are strong supporters of education, housing, business, and economic development.

The official Web site of the Cherokee nation notes: "It was a spirit of survival and perseverance that carried the Cherokee to Indian Territory on the Trail of Tears. Today, it is the same spirit leading the Cherokee."

This painting shows Cherokee Indians being forced to move to new lands west of the Mississippi River during the late 1830s.

The Legendary Bruce Lee

Bruce Lee was born in San Francisco, California, on November 27, 1940. His family moved to Hong Kong a year later. When he was 12, Lee was beaten by a street gang. To protect himself from future beatings, he decided to learn martial arts.

After returning to the United States in 1959, Lee opened several kung fu schools. He landed the role of Kato in the 1966 television series *Green Hornet*, based on a comic book character. Though he was only playing the sidekick, Lee turned out to be more popular than the lead actor!

Eventually, Lee decided to return to Hong Kong. The market for kung fu movies was much better there. *Fists of Fury*, released in Hong Kong in 1971, boosted him to instant fame. His astonishing high kicks and graceful moves won his fans over. This film was followed by *The Chinese Connection* and *Return of the Dragon* in 1972.

Bruce Lee passed away suddenly on July 20, 1973. He was in the midst of filming a movie that was eventually released as *Enter the Dragon*. The cause of death was excessive fluid in the brain, most likely from an allergic reaction to aspirin. He was just 32 years old.

"If I should die tomorrow," Lee once said, "I will have no regrets. I did what I wanted to do. You can't expect more from life." Today, Bruce Lee is regarded as one of the most influential martial artists of all time.

This statue of martial arts icon Bruce Lee stands in Hong Kong's Victoria Harbor.

Popular Martial Arts for Kids

Judo, karate, and tae kwon do are popular styles of martial arts. How can someone choose the style that is right for them?

Judo is Japanese for "the gentle way." The main idea is to bring the other person to the ground by using their weight and strength against them, rather than using your own. It can be a good choice for people who are just starting out, especially younger children. Judo builds balance and coordination with minimal risk of injury.

Karate means "empty hand" in Japanese. It involves no weapons, and is traditionally fought with bare hands and feet. Karate includes striking with the hands or elbows as well as kicking. It requires a great deal of fitness and skill to become a karate champion. But it is still an easy style for beginners to pick up, especially for older kids and teens.

Tae kwon do is a Korean martial art similar to karate. It roughly means "foot-hand way." In addition to kicking and striking with the hands, tae kwon do features many jumping moves. It has a stronger emphasis on using the foot compared to karate. It is a popular choice among older kids and teens, although even very young children practice it.

People of all ages study these styles, and many others. The martial arts are truly for everyone!

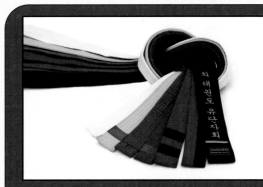

In many martial arts, different-colored belts are awarded as students achieve higher levels of skill.

The Vietnam War

In 1959, a military conflict erupted in Southeast Asia between North Vietnam, which was ruled by a communist government, and South Vietnam. South Vietnam was supported by the United States, which began sending troops to fight in Vietnam during the mid-1960s. The American effort failed. Vietnam was reunited under communist rule in 1975. The toll on human life included about 3.5 million Vietnamese, 2 million Laotians and Cambodians, and 58,000 U.S. soldiers.

Many Americans questioned the reasons behind U.S. involvement in Vietnam. This led to anti-war protests. Veterans returning home from Vietnam were jeered by angry crowds, rather than cheered. This marked the first time Americans were so deeply divided over a war.

Another difficult issue involved soldiers who were still in Vietnam. During the conflict, about 2,500 Americans had been held as prisoners of war. But were all of them returned after the fighting ended? This question has nagged many people since 1973, when the North Vietnamese released about 600 servicemen from captivity. Some believe the communists kept other prisoners as bargaining chips in return for U.S. funds to help rebuild their war-torn country. More than 30 years later, the search continues for information about U.S. personnel missing in action in Vietnam.

The "Three Servicemen" statue at the Vietnam Veterans Memorial in Washington, D.C., honors Americans who served in Vietnam.

"Best of the Best"

When a military emergency arises that must be handled quickly, Delta Force often gets the assignment. It is known as the 1st Special Operational Detachment—Delta. U.S. Army Colonel Charles Beckwith first organized the unit in 1977. Modeled after the British Special Air Service (SAS), the members are highly trained to handle any dangerous situation. Delta Force specializes in counterterrorism operations worldwide. They have performed numerous top secret missions.

During the 1980s, Delta Force had missions in Iran, Grenada, Bolivia, the Persian Gulf, Africa, and Panama. In October 1993, the unit was sent to Somalia. While attempting to locate and capture two rebels, a Black Hawk helicopter was shot down. Two Delta Force members, Master Sergeant Gary Gordon and Sergeant First Class Randall Shughart, were killed while defending the crash site.

More recently, Delta Force has served in Iraq and Afghanistan. It works closely with the local population to eliminate terrorists.

Members join this elite unit by invitation only. Most are taken from among the Special Forces units of all the branches of the U.S. military, such as the Army Rangers, Green Berets, and Navy SEALs. These are just some of the reasons why many refer to them as the "best of the best."

Rugged Bunch

Since their humble beginning in 1823, the Texas Rangers have grown to become one of the most illustrious law enforcement agencies in the United States. In their early days, the Rangers' main duties were to protect settlers from outlaws and attacks by certain Native American tribes. It was not until the 1870s that the Texas Rangers really began to organize. Enlistments usually lasted for a year. The pay was $1.25 per day.

Armed with Colt revolvers and repeating rifles, this rugged bunch of frontiersmen brought law and order to the Lone Star State. But as times changed, so did the Rangers. They kept a close eye on the border with Mexico during World War I. From 1920 to 1933, Prohibition outlawed the making and selling of alcohol in the United States. The Texas Rangers helped track down bootleggers who continued the trade illegally. They chased bandits, including the infamous Bonnie and Clyde, during the 1930s.

In recent years, the Texas Rangers have continued to adapt to the high-tech world of modern law enforcement. Computers, updated forensic techniques, and current crime-fighting methods have improved their capabilities. Today, several companies of Texas Rangers are located across the state. They are a proud organization with a rich tradition.

This statue of a Texas Ranger guards the state capitol building in Austin.

Making Dreams Come True

The Make-A-Wish Foundation has been making dreams come true for thousands of sick children since 1980. It all began when seven-year-old Christopher Greicius had his wish fulfilled when he got a ride in a police helicopter. He was also sworn in as an Arizona Department of Public Safety officer, complete his own uniform and hat. Sadly, Chris died a few days later of leukemia.

Since that time, the organization has helped many other kids. How does it work? Children from two-and-a-half to 18 years old who have been diagnosed with a serious, life-threatening illness by a physician are eligible. One of the many "wish teams" will visit the child to find out his or her most passionate desire. The group then makes arrangements with other individuals and businesses to help make that wish become a reality.

The foundation has granted wishes to more than 170,000 kids around the globe. As the program grows, its original mission remains intact: "We grant the wishes of children with life-threatening medical conditions to enrich the human experience with hope, strength and joy." That is a mission worth working for!

Chuck and Gina Norris pose with four children who asked to meet the action star through the Make-A-Wish Foundation.

Chronology

1940: Carlos Ray Norris is born on March 10 in Ryan, Oklahoma.

1958: Norris enlists in the U.S. Air Force in August. Marries Dianne Holechek.

1959: Transferred to South Korea for one year, during which time he becomes a black belt in tang soo do.

1962: Discharged from the Air Force. Son Mike is born.

1964: Norris begins teaching karate full-time in his studios. Son Eric is born.

1967: Wins the All-American Grand Championship in New York. Wins the International Grand Championship in Long Beach, California.

1968: Wins the International Grand Championship in Long Beach, California. Wins the World Professional Middleweight Karate Championship, a title he will hold undefeated until his retirement in 1974.

1970: Norris's brother Wieland is killed in Vietnam on June 3. Norris and business partner Bob Wall sell their schools, but continue on as instructors.

1972: Appears in *Return of the Dragon* with Bruce Lee. Norris's father, Ray, is killed in a car accident.

1973: Norris buys his schools back to protect them from mismanagement, then resells them to protect them from going bankrupt.

1974: Retires from professional karate competition as the unde-feated middleweight champion.

1978: *Good Guys Wear Black* is released.

1980: Norris becomes actively involved with the Make-A-Wish Foundation.

1984: *Missing in Action* is released.

1989: Norris and his wife, Dianne, divorce.

1990: The Kick Drugs Out of America Foundation is founded on August 16. The name will change to KickStart in 1993. Names the martial arts style he developed *chun kuk do,* or "the universal way."

1993: First episode of *Walker, Texas Ranger* airs on April 21; the show will run for nine seasons, with a follow-up television movie in 2005.

1998: Norris marries Gena O'Kelley on November 28.

2001: Twin son and daughter Dakota Alan and Danilee Kelley are born on August 30.

2008: Norris campaigns on behalf of Republican presidential candidate Mike Huckabee.

Accomplishments/Awards
Films

The Wrecking Crew (1969)
Return of the Dragon (1972)
Breaker! Breaker! (1977)
Good Guys Wear Black (1978)
A Force of One (1979)
The Octagon (1980)
An Eye for an Eye (1981)
Silent Rage (1982)
Forced Vengeance (1982)
Lone Wolf McQuade (1983)
Missing in Action (1984)
Missing in Action 2: The
    Beginning (1985)
Code of Silence (1985)
Invasion U.S.A. (1985)

The Delta Force (1986)
Firewalker (1986)
Braddock: Missing in Action
    III (1988)
Hero and the Terror (1988)
Delta Force 2: The Colombian
    Connection (Operation
    Stranglehold) (1990)
The Hitman (1991)
Sidekicks (1993)
Hellbound (1994)
Top Dog (1995)
Forrest Warrior (video) (1996)
Bells of Innocence (2003)
The Cutter (2005)

Television

Walker, Texas Ranger (1993-
    2001)
Wind in the Wire (1993)
Logan's War: Bound By Honor
    (1998)

The President's Man (2000)
The President's Man: A Line in
    the Sand (2002)
Walker, Texas Ranger: Trial by
    Fire (2005)

Books by Chuck Norris

Winning Tournament Karate (1975)

The Secret of Inner Strength: My Story, with Joe Hyams (1989)

The Secret Power Within: Zen Solutions to Real Problems (1996)

Against All Odds: My Story, with Ken Abraham (2004)

The Justice Riders, with Ken Abraham, Aaron Norris, and Tim Grayem (2006)

A Threat to Justice: A Novel, with Ken Abraham, Aaron Norris, and Tim Grayem (2007)

Black Belt Patriotism: How to Reawaken America (2008)

Further Reading

Cole, Melanie. *Chuck Norris*. Childs, Md.: Mitchell Lane
    Publishers, 1999.

Crudelli, Chris. *The Way of the Warrior: Martial Arts and Fighting
    Styles From Around the World*. New York: DK Publishing, 2008.

Norris, Chuck, with Ken Abraham. *Against All Odds: My Story*.
    Nashville, Tennessee: Broadman & Holman Publishers, 2004.

Smeds, Dave. *Chuck Norris*. New York: Rosen Publishing Group,
    2002.

Internet Resources

http://www.chucknorris.com

The official Web site for Chuck Norris.

http://www.kick-start.org

Information about the KickStart program Norris founded
in 1990.

**http://www.worldblackbelt.com/Martial_Arts_Styles/Martial_
Arts_Styles.asp**

Online site with descriptions of various types of martial arts.

http://www.imdb.com/

The Internet Movie Database, which includes a list of all
of Norris's film and television accomplishments.

Glossary

advocate—one who supports a person, group, or cause.

black belt—the highest level of achievement in many martial arts.

conservative—supporting traditional views, especially in politics.

gratuitous—uncalled for or unnecessary; extra.

humanitarian—working for or supporting efforts to help those in need.

integrity—having good values; honest.

investor—one who provides money to support a business or cause.

leukemia—a form of cancer common among children.

malaria—a dangerous disease spread by mosquitoes that is common in certain areas of the world.

martial arts—"arts of war," fighting styles developed for use in war, self-defense, or other such reasons. Examples include judo, karate, kung fu, tang soo do, and tae kwon do.

nonprofit—not for profit or money.

paternal—fatherly; related to fatherhood.

patriotism—a strong belief in one's country.

reflexive—automatic; done without thinking.

veteran—someone with experience, especially someone who has served in the military.

Chapter Notes

p. 8: "I said that I felt ..." Norris and Abraham, *Against All Odds: My Story* (Nashville: Broadman & Holman Publishers, 2004), 155.

p. 10: "A sense of belonging ..." "Program Overview: Key Strategies," KickStart. http://www.kick-start.org/strategies.html.

p. 11: "If I had accepted ..." Norris and Abraham, *Against All Odds*, 245.

p. 12: "She was the most ..." Chuck Norris with Joe Hyams, *The Secret of Inner Strength: My Story* (Boston: Little, Brown and Company, 1988), 13.

p. 14: "Confronting Bobby the bully ..." Norris and Abraham, *Against All Odds*, 16.

p. 14: "I discovered a new pride ..." Ibid., 28.

p. 15: "I was shy..." Ira Berkow, "At Dinner With: Chuck Norris; When That 97-Pound Weakling Grows Up," *New York Times*, May 12, 1993. http://query.nytimes.com/gst/fullpage.html?res=9F0CE0DE 103CF931A25756C0A965958260.

p. 17: "Looking back, I realize ..." Chuck Norris, *The Secret Power Within: Zen Solutions to Real Problems* (Boston: Little, Brown and Company, 1996), 15.

p. 19: "The matches were hotly contested ..." Norris and Abraham, *Against All Odds*, 52.

p. 20: "The key here is practice ..." Chuck Norris, *Winning Tournament Karate*, (Santa Clarita, Calif.: Ohara Publications, 1975), 16.

p. 21: "I know why he was ..." Norris, *The Secret Power Within*, 181–182.

p. 23:   "For the first time ..." Norris and Abraham, *Against All Odds*, 84.

p. 24:   "You've got this intensity ..." Berkow, *New York Times*.

p. 29:   "Aaron jumped into a boat ..." Norris and Abraham, *Against All Odds*, 132.

p. 30:   *Code of Silence* is a thriller ..." Roger Ebert, "Code of Silence," *Chicago Sun-Times*, May 3, 1985. http://rogerebert.suntimes.com/ apps/pbcs.dll/article?AID=/19850503/REVIEWS/505030301/1023.

p. 32:   "I don't like violence ..." Berkow, *New York Times*.

p. 32:   "I'm not Superman ..." Ibid.

p. 34:   "You had enough action ..." Jay Bobbin, "Chuck Norris Sees Action Again," TV.com, October 15, 2005. http://www.tv.com/ tracking/ viewer.html?tid=73861&ref_id=244&ref_type=101&om_act= convert&om_clk=headlinessh&tag=headlines;title;3.

p. 39:   "I went to her ..." Norris and Abraham, *Against All Odds*, 173.

p. 41:   "Danilee and Dakota ..." Ibid., 222.

p. 46:   "He's an American institution ..." "What people have said about John Wayne," JWayne.com. http://www.jwayne.com/ unforgettable_jwayne.shtml.

p. 47:   "It was a spirit of ..." Cherokee Nation Cultural Resource Center, "A Brief History of the Cherokee Nation: A Proud Heritage," Cherokee Nation. http://www.cherokee.org/ Culture/57/Page/default.aspx.

p. 48:   "If I should die tomorrow ..." Jake Seal, "The Mystery of Bruce Lee's Death," All About Bruce Lee. http://www.allbrucelee.com/article/ mystery_of_bruce_lee.htm.

p. 53:   "We grant the wishes ..." Make-A-Wish Foundation of America, "Our Mission," Make-A-Wish Foundation. http://www.wish.org/about/our_mission.

Index

Numbers in **bold italics** refer to captions.

Photo Credits

About the Author

Connecticut native **AL HEMINGWAY** is currently the book review editor for *Military Heritage* magazine. Many of his articles have appeared in magazines such as *World War II History, Vietnam, Military History,* and *America's Civil War.* His book *Our War Was Different: Marine Combined Action Platoons in Vietnam* was published by Naval Institute Press in 1994. He is also a regular contributor to the commentary page of the *Waterbury Republican-American,* writing on military and historical topics.